BREAKING FREE
FROM...

By Nadine Cepeda-Carr

Scripture quotations are taken from the *Holy Bible*, New Living Translation, copyright ©1996, 2004, 2015 by Tyndale House Foundation. Used by permission of Tyndale House Publishers, Carol Stream, Illinois 60188. All rights reserved.

Book design by: Larisma Dellareese Maduro
Edited by: Spirit of Excellence Writing & Editing Services, LLC

ISBN 979-8-218-07923-9 (paperback)
First paperback edition October 2022
Published by Shedding Light Ministries LLC

CONTACT INFORMATION

shedding1light@gmail.com
www.sheddinglightministries.com

Please feel free to contact me for
speaking engagements for your church,
workshops, conferences, small groups, and retreats.

Table of Contents

Introduction

What is Freedom?

What does the word freedom mean to you?

_____

_____

_____

When was the last time you felt free?

_____

_____

_____

What are you wanting to be set free from?

_____

_____

_____

What are you expecting to get out of this book?

_____

_____

_____

Chapter 1
Breaking Free from
Unforgiveness

Please complete chapter one in your textbook before moving on to the next chapter of this book

Who do you need to forgive?

_____

_____

_____

Do you need to forgive yourself? _____ If your answer is yes, why do you need to forgive yourself?

_____

_____

_____

What feelings are rising as you answer these questions?

_____

_____

_____

Here are some questions that may be going through your mind right now:

1. How do I know when I have truly forgiven that person?

• When it no longer hurts you, makes you angry, or affects you the way it did before

• When you can speak about it freely

• When you now have compassion towards the person who hurt you

• When you can pray for that person and be sincere about it

For those of you who need to forgive yourself for something wrong you did

2. How do I know I have forgiven myself?

• When you no longer carry guilt, shame, or condemnation - Romans 8:1 says, "So now there is no condemnation for those who belong to Christ Jesus"
• You will feel completely free and at peace

PRAY: Father, help me to forgive those who have hurt me and bring to the surface any unforgiveness I may be carrying that has been hidden and lying dormant in me. Your word says if I cannot forgive them, you will not forgive me. I ask that You bring me healing for every pain and hurt I may have encountered by others. Mend every broken piece of my heart and help me to identify and not hold on to any bitterness or anger towards them. Please help me so that I may release it and place it at your feet in Jesus' name, Amen.

NOTES

(Take this time to meditate and write down what God is speaking and revealing to you about this topic)

Chapter 2
Breaking Free from
Rejection

Please complete chapter two in your textbook before moving on to the next chapter of this book

Before answering the following questions, really dig deep internally within yourself.

Who in your life have you been rejected by?

_____

_____

_____

What outcomes have taken place due to your rejection?

_____

_____

_____

How has it affected you?

_____

_____

_____

Read the following scriptures regarding God's love for us.

The Prodigal Son in Luke 15:11-31 - That same love He has for His Son, He has for us.

Luke 15:4 - If a man has a hundred sheep and one of them gets lost, what will He do? Won't He leave the ninety-nine others in the wilderness and go search for the one that is lost until He finds it?

Romans 5:8 - But God showed His great love for us by sending Christ to die for us while we were still sinners.

John 3:16- For this is how God loved the world: He gave His one and only Son, so that everyone who believes in Him will not perish but have eternal life. God sent His Son into the world not to judge the world, but to save the world through Him.

PRAY: Father, I cast down the spirit of rejection, every person who hurt and disappointed me. Father, I ask You to bring healing to the deepest part of my wounded soul. Help me to know that I am loved and accepted by You. It does not matter what anyone else says or thinks about me; what matters is what You say about me and how You see me. Thank You for loving me unconditionally and accepting me just as I am. No one can love me the way that You do. I thank you for giving up Your Son to die on the cross just for me and showing me how much I am loved by you in Jesus' name, Amen.

NOTES

_____

_____

_____

_____

_____

_____

_____

_____

_____

_____

_____

_____

_____

_____

_____

_____

_____

Chapter 3
Breaking Free from
Fear

Please complete chapter three in your textbook before moving on to the next chapter of this book

---

FEAR: Forever Expecting Awful Results

Fear is a stronghold that many people deal with. It can keep you bound in many ways. Here are just a few ways:

- Fear of failure
- Fear of change
- Fear of the unknown
- Fear of sickness
- Fear of loss
- Fear of what people will think or say about you
- Fear of disappointments
- Fear of setbacks
- Fear of not being accepted
- Fear of rejection

Take a moment to think about the fears you have been dealing with:

What are your fears?

_____

_____

_____

_____

What have been your results from the fears you have been carrying?

_____

_____

_____

What fears are you ready to let go?

_____

_____

_____

_____

Fear must GO now in Jesus' name! Fear does not come from God; it comes from Satan. God's word says...

2 Timothy 1:7 - For God has not given us a spirit of fear and timidity, but of power, love, and self- discipline.

Isaiah 41:10 - Don't be afraid, for I am with you. Don't be discouraged, for I am your God. I will strengthen you and help you. I will hold you up with my victorious right hand.

Philippians 4:13 - For I can do everything through Christ, who gives me strength.

We are to fear God only but never in a bad way.

1 John 4:18 - Such love has no fear, because perfect love expels all fear. If we are afraid, it is for fear of punishment, and this shows that we have not fully experienced His perfect love.

Proverbs 9:10 - Fear of the Lord is the foundation of wisdom. Knowledge of the Holy One results in good judgment.

PRAY: Father, I cast down all fear and I ask You to please fill me with Your peace, rest and comfort. For Your word says that You have not given us the spirit of fear but of power, love, and a sound mind. I call forth (name your fear) _____ and anything that I'm not aware of that is attached to it; this must go right now in Jesus' name. May You replace it with Your boldness and a stronger faith and hope in Jesus' name, Amen.

NOTES

(Take this time to meditate and write down what God is speaking and revealing to you about this topic)

Since we are on the topic about fear, let us speak on FAITH over fear.

FAITH: **F**ull **A**ssurance **I**n **T**he **H**eart

Would you say you have faith? If not, then why?

_____

_____

_____

In what areas of your life do you need to build your faith?

_____

_____

_____

What caused you to lose your faith? Think back to what happened and when.

_____

_____

_____

Hebrews 11:1 - Faith shows the reality of what we hope for; it is the evidence of things we cannot see.

Read Hebrews 11 - it shows great examples of faith.

If you ever heard of the story of David and Goliath, this is a true story of faith. David was a small boy who killed this giant named Goliath with only one stone (he had five) when bigger and stronger soldiers in the army were discouraged and scared to come against Him. God has given us our own personal stones to overcome the giants in our lives. The five stones God has given us are the Holy Spirit, prayer, worship, scripture, and wisdom.

Read 1 Samuel 17

Faith comes by hearing and hearing by the word of God. The more you feed your spirit man within you, the more your faith will grow; this happens by feeding yourself the word of God.

Read Romans 10:17

Faith and hope go hand and hand. You cannot have hope without faith and vice versa. Faith means trusting, not by what you see but believing with hope that whatever you have been praying for that it will happen.

Are you feeding your spirit man or your soul? What you feed grows and what you starve dies. Decide today what you want to feed and what you want to starve.

PRAY: Father, I pray and ask that You may help me with my unbelief. In the areas where I lack faith, may you help to increase it. I command the spirits of lies and discouragement that try to flood my mind and heart to leave me right now in Jesus' name. May you pour out on to me a fresh hope, fresh faith, and your spirit as I grow closer and closer to you so I may trust in you more and more each day in Jesus' name, Amen.

NOTES

(Take this time to meditate and write down what God is speaking and revealing to you about this topic)

Chapter 4
Breaking Free from
Anger

Please complete chapter four in your textbook before moving on to the next chapter of this book

We also must pay close attention when we get angry at someone. Is it rage or a normal angry feeling?

Can you remember the last time you got angry/enraged? What was your response?

_____

_____

_____

How did your anger manifest?

_____

_____

_____

What was the outcome after your outburst?

_____

_____

_____

Ephesians 6:12 - For we are not fighting against flesh-and-blood enemies, but against evil rulers and authorities of the unseen world, against mighty powers in this dark world, and against evil spirits in the heavenly places.

Let us remember what we are really fighting against. We are not fighting flesh but against principalities.

The book of Galatians speaks about the fruit of the Spirit. This passage of scripture reminds us how we should be walking:

Galatians 5:22-23 - But the Holy Spirit produces this kind of fruit in our lives: love, joy, peace, patience, kindness, goodness, faithfulness, gentleness, and self-control. There is no law against these things!

PRAY: Father, I lift this anger to You. As I place it at Your feet, may You replace it with Your joy and peace. May You fill me up with Your love so that I may love and have compassion towards those who may have hurt me. May You reveal to me the root of this anger and as You do that, I will present it back to You. Create in me a clean heart so any anger in me may not hinder me in Jesus' name, Amen.

NOTES

_____

_____

_____

_____

_____

_____

_____

_____

_____

_____

_____

_____

_____

_____

_____

_____

Chapter 5
Breaking Free from
Depression

Please complete chapter five in your textbook before moving on to the next chapter of this book

Do you deal with depression? If yes, how do you deal with it?

_____

_____

_____

In what way does your depression manifest?

_____

_____

_____

How do you handle your depression? What actions do you take?

_____

_____

_____

Here are some encouraging scriptures that will remind you in times of discouragement and hopelessness how good and faithful God is and how close He is to the brokenhearted:

Proverbs 12:25 - Worry weighs a person down; an encouraging word cheers a person up.

Deuteronomy 31:8 - Do not be afraid or discouraged, for the Lord will personally go ahead of you. He will be with you; He will neither fail you nor abandon you."

Psalm 9:9 - The Lord is a shelter for the oppressed, a refuge in times of trouble.

Psalm 34:18-19 - The Lord is close to the brokenhearted; He rescues those whose spirits are crushed. The righteous person faces many troubles, but the Lord comes to the rescue each time.

Psalm 126:5 - Those who plant in tears will harvest with shouts of joy.

Romans 15:13 - I pray that God, the source of hope, will fill you completely with joy and peace because you trust in Him. Then you will overflow with confident hope through the power of the Holy Spirit.

PRAY: Father, I lift depression right now to You, Lord. May you fill me with an everlasting joy. Your word says that You will give me beauty for ashes, the oil of joy for mourning and the garment of praise for the spirit of heaviness; that I might be called a tree of righteousness, the planting of the Lord, that He might be glorified. Pour down Your joy that I may be filled with laughter in Jesus' name, Amen.

NOTES

(Take this time to meditate and write down what God is speaking and revealing to you about this topic)

Chapter 6
Breaking Free from
Lust

Please complete chapter six in your textbook before moving on to the next chapter of this book

What is the first thing you think about when you hear the word lust?

_____

_____

_____

Here are two definitions:

- A passionate or overmastering desire or craving, or a lust for power

- Having a very strong sexual desire for someone

Read the following scriptures that speak on "do not love this world."

1 John 2:15-17 - Do not love this world nor the things it offers you, for when you love the world, you do not have the love of the Father in you. For the world offers only a craving for physical pleasure, a craving for everything we see, and pride in our achievements and possessions. These are not from the Father but are from this world. And this world is fading away, along with everything that people crave. But anyone who does what pleases God will live forever.

Galatians 5:16 - So I say, let the Holy Spirit guide your lives. Then you won't be doing what your sinful nature craves.

Colossians 3:5 - So put to death the sinful, earthly things lurking within you. Have nothing to do with sexual immorality, impurity, lust, and evil desires. Don't be greedy, for a greedy person is an idolater, worshiping the things of this world.

1 Thessalonians 4:3-5 - God's will is for you to be holy, so stay away from all sexual sin. Then each of you will control his own body and live in holiness and honor not in lustful passion like the pagans who do not know God and His ways.

Sexual Soul Ties

Stop and think as we speak on this topic. Can you think of any sexual soul ties you might still have from your past or even now? Write the names down.

_____

_____

_____

Can you think of any unhealthy soul ties you may still have from your past or even now? Write the names down.

_____

_____

_____

How to know if you have an ungodly soul tie:

Take a moment in prayer and ask God to show you if you have soul ties that need to be severed. If the Lord brings people to mind or you think there is a possibility of a soul tie, proceed to pray to cut the soul ties. It may or may not happen in one prayer. It can be so deeply buried that you do not remember but in God's timing, he will bring names to the surface or even a memory of that person. Each time the Lord brings it to the surface, start to renounce those soul ties with the prayer shared below.

PRAY: To break soul ties:

Father God, I thank You for saving me from destruction. I thank You for sending Jesus to die for my sins. Please forgive me for my sins against You. Specifically, I confess that I _____ (details of the sin and names). I repent of that sin and renounce it now.

Lord, please purify my heart from this sin, the memory of it and any fantasy I have entertained in my mind regarding it. In the name of Jesus Christ and by the power of His blood that was shed on the cross, I cut myself free from every soul tie that took place with _____ (name (s) or specific objects).

25

I commit him/her/them to the care of Jesus Christ for Him to do with as He wills. Satan, I rebuke you and all Your works and ways. I rebuke any evil spirits that have a stronghold in me. In the name of Jesus, I command you evil spirits to leave me and go back to the pit of hell where you belong. Father, please heal my soul of any wounds resulting from these soul ties. Please restore any part of me that have been stolen through this/these soul tie(s) and bring me back again to wholeness. Refresh my soul and rebuild me back to the person you created me to be. Thank you, Lord, for Your healing power and your perfect love for me. May I glorify You with my life from this point forward in Jesus' name, Amen.

NOTES

(Take this time to meditate and write down what God is speaking and revealing to you about this topic)

Chapter 7
Breaking Free from
Identity

Please complete chapter seven in your textbook before moving on to the next chapter of this book

---

The definition of identity is the fact of being who or what a person or thing is.

This reminds me of identity theft: When someone steals another person's identity like a social security number or a physical ID their intent is to create a new identity for themselves. They are trying to be someone they are not. The same happens internally with people after trauma; something shifts inside them and creates a different person whom God did not create originally.

Here are some scriptures that speak about your identity:

Ephesians 1:5-7 - God decided in advance to adopt us into His own family by bringing us to Himself through Jesus Christ. This is what He wanted to do, and it gave Him great pleasure. So we praise God for the glorious grace He has poured out on us who belong to His dear Son. He is so rich in kindness and grace that He purchased our freedom with the blood of His Son and forgave our sins.

1 Corinthians 12:27 - All of you together are Christ's body, and each of you is a part of it.

Jeremiah 1:5 - I knew you before I formed you in your mother's womb. Before you were born I set you apart and appointed you as my prophet to the nations.

1 Corinthians 6:19-20 - Don't you realize that your body is the temple of the Holy Spirit, who lives in you and was given to you by God? You do not belong to yourself, for God bought you with a high price. So you must honor God with your body.

1 Corinthians 6:17 - But the person who is joined to the Lord is one spirit with Him.

Genesis 1:27 - So God created human beings in His own image. In the image of God, He created them; male and female He created them.

In your prayer time, ask God, where is my identity? Who have I been all these years?

PRAY: Father, as You reveal to me how I have been living my life all these years without You and the identity I have taken over I ask that You wipe it away. Replace it with Your DNA and the identity that You have given me so I may walk in my true calling and purpose You have for me. I am wonderfully made in Your image. Thank You for creating me to be who You have called me to be in Jesus' name, Amen.

NOTES

(Take this time to meditate and write down what God is speaking and revealing to you about this topic)

Chapter 8
Breaking Free from
Infirmity

Please complete chapter eight in your textbook before moving on to the next chapter of this book

In your moment of despair during a sickness you encountered, was your faith shook?

_____

_____

_____

Did fear grip you?

_____

_____

_____

What lies were Satan whispering in your ear?

_____

_____

_____

Were you able to still look to God and worship Him during your hopelessness?

_____

_____

_____

Luke 8:43-48 - A woman in the crowd had suffered for twelve years with constant bleeding, and she could find no cure. Coming up behind Jesus, she touched the fringe of His robe.

Immediately, the bleeding stopped. "Who touched me?" Jesus asked. Everyone denied it, and Peter said, "Master, this whole crowd is pressing up against You." But Jesus said, "Someone deliberately touched me, for I felt healing power go out from me." When the woman realized that she could not stay hidden, she began to tremble and fell to her knees in front of Him. The whole crowd heard her explain why she had touched Him and that she had been immediately healed. "Daughter," He said to her, "your faith has made you well. Go in peace."

Here are two other stories on how Jesus healed a lame man and a blind man. Nothing is too hard or impossible for our God when it comes to healing the sick. I believe it's a way to show the miracle of God to those who have unbelief.

John 5:1-9- Afterward Jesus returned to Jerusalem for one of the Jewish holy days. Inside the city, near the Sheep Gate, was the pool of Bethesda, with five covered porches. Crowds of sick people—blind, lame, or paralyzed-lay on the porches. One of the men lying there had been sick for thirty-eight years. When Jesus saw him and knew He had been ill for a long time, He asked him, "Would you like to get well?" "I can't, sir," the sick man said, "for I have no one to put me into the pool when the water bubbles up. Someone else always gets there ahead of me." Jesus told him, "Stand up, pick up your mat, and walk!" Instantly, the man was healed! He rolled up his sleeping mat and began walking! But this miracle happened on the Sabbath.

John 9:1-7- As Jesus was walking along, He saw a man who had been blind from birth. "Rabbi," His disciples asked Him, "why was this man born blind? Was it because of his own sins or his parents' sins?" "It was not because of his sins or his parents' sins," Jesus answered. "This happened so the power of God could be seen in him. We must quickly carry out the tasks assigned us by the one who sent us. The night is coming, and then no one can work. But while I am here in the world, I am the light of the world." Then he spit on the ground, made mud with the saliva, and spread the mud over the blind man's eyes. He told him, "Go wash yourself in the pool of Siloam" (Siloam means "sent"). So, the man went and washed and came back seeing!

Here are just a few scriptures to speak over yourself when you're sick. The Bible is full of scriptures that encourage us and fill us with hope, peace, and rest. Speak it into the atmosphere and into existence. Remember, there is power in your words. Start thanking God for your healing as if it's already done.

Isaiah 41:10 - Don't be afraid, for I am with you. Don't be discouraged, for I am Your God. I will strengthen you and help you. I will hold you up with my victorious right hand

Psalm 30:2 - O Lord my God, I cried to You for help, and You restored my health.

Matthew 11:28-30 - Then Jesus said, "Come to me, all of you who are weary and carry heavy burdens, and I will give you rest. Take my yoke upon you. Let me teach you, because I am humble and gentle at heart, and you will find rest for your souls. For my yoke is easy to bear, and the burden I give you is light."

Romans 15:13 - I pray that God, the source of hope, will fill you completely with joy and peace because you trust in Him. Then you will overflow with confident hope through the power of the Holy Spirit.

Psalm 46:1 - God is our refuge and strength, always ready to help in times of trouble.

PRAY: Father, I lift every sickness in my body, everything known and unknown. You are an all-knowing God. I pray and ask You to cover me with the blood of Jesus from the top of my head to the soles of my feet. I plead the blood of Jesus over every organ, muscle, vessel, and bone in my body. I claim physical healing; may You restore my body back to how You intended it to be - in good health. Fill me with Your Holy Spirit and as You fill me up, it will leave no room for the spirit of infirmity. Sickness has no choice but to leave my body in Jesus' name. I thank You in advance for my healing. I'm believing in faith that You have made me whole in Jesus' name Amen.

NOTES

(Take this time to meditate and write down what God is speaking and revealing to you about this topic)

Chapter 9
Breaking Free from
Shame & Guilt

Please complete chapter nine in your textbook before moving on to the next chapter of this book

What have you done in your past that has caused you shame or guilt?

_____

_____

_____

Do you have someone who constantly reminds you of your mistakes?

_____

_____

_____

How does it make you feel?

_____

_____

_____

Do you truly think God can forgive you for what you have done?

_____

_____

_____

Ask God to forgive you for (fill in the blank).

_____

_____

_____

Read what God says in the following scriptures:

Psalm 130:3 - Lord, if You kept a record of our sins, who, O Lord, could ever survive?

Jeremiah 31:34 - And they will not need to teach their neighbors, nor will they need to teach their relatives, saying, 'You should know the Lord.' For everyone, from the least to the greatest, will know me already," says the Lord. "And I will forgive their wickedness, and I will never again remember their sins."

Romans 8:1 - So now there is no condemnation for those who belong to Christ Jesus.

Shame was never a God-intended emotion. In fact, the Bible says that the enemy is the accuser of believers - meaning that the voice that tries to shame us, minimize who we are, and steal our confidence is from the enemy. God will never bring shame to you. He corrects and restores His children with love.

Hebrews 12:5 – And have you forgotten the encouraging words God spoke to you as His children? He said, "My child, don't make light of the Lord's discipline, and don't give up when He corrects you.

PRAY: Father, I lay at Your feet every guilt and shame from my past. You have forgiven me and have washed me clean with the blood of Jesus. When I accepted You in my life, You erased my past and gave me a new life. The old has died and I am now a new person. I command the enemy's mouth to be shut each time my past is brought up. Thank You for seeing me as the finished project and thank You for loving me unconditionally in Jesus' name, Amen.

NOTES

(Take this time to meditate and write down what God is speaking and revealing to you about this topic)

Chapter 10
Breaking Free from
Your Mindset

Please complete chapter ten in your textbook

What negative thoughts constantly play in your mind?

_____

_____

_____

How has this caused you to move forward in your actions?

_____

_____

_____

Here are some ways you can begin to renew your mind with the mind of Christ:

Having the mind of Christ means we look at life from God's point of view. His thoughts are not like the way the world thinks. His values and His desires in mind towards us are totally different from our own. His perspective of humility, compassion, and dependence He wants us to have the same.

We can lay hands on our minds and pray, asking God to bind our mind to the mind of Christ. We need to ask God to renew our mind daily. We don't have to wait to have someone pray over your mind, you can do it yourself. God has given you the power and authority to take captive over your thoughts. Ask God to give your mind peace, rest, and a sound mind. The mind of Christ is given to you through the Holy Spirit.

1 Corinthians 2:10-12 - But it was to us that God revealed these things by His Spirit. For His Spirit searches out everything and shows us God's deep secrets. No one can know a person's thoughts except that person's own spirit, and no one can know God's thoughts except God's own Spirit. And we have received God's Spirit (not the world's spirit), so we can know the wonderful things God has freely given us.

Romans 12:2 - Don't copy the behavior and customs of this world, but let God transform you into a new person by changing the way you think. Then you will learn to know God's will for you, which is good and pleasing and perfect.

Philippians 2:5 - You must have the same attitude that Christ Jesus had.

2 Timothy 1:7 - For God has not given us a spirit of fear and timidity, but of power, love, and self- discipline.

Ephesians 4:23-24 - Instead, let the Spirit renew your thoughts and attitudes. Put on your new nature, created to be like God—truly righteous and Holy.

Pray over your mind and start declaring God's word over your mind. Let's start breaking these patterns and old ways of thinking.

PRAY: Father, I bind my mind to Your mind; let every thought that is not coming from You be held captive. Uproot, break, and bind every old way of thinking and renew my mind. May my mind be transformed to Your ways. Please give me a mind of peace, rest and soundness in Jesus' name, Amen.

NOTES

www.ingramcontent.com/pod-product-compliance
Lightning Source LLC
Chambersburg PA
CBHW082113120626
46553CB00011B/3664